T0011852

BLUE SKIES AND GOLDEN FIELDS

CELEBRATING UKRAINE

BY OKSANA LUSHCHEVSKA

CAPSTONE PRESS
a capstone imprint

Published by Capstone Press, an imprint of Capstone
1710 Roe Crest Drive, North Mankato, Minnesota 56003
capstonepub.com

Library of Congress Cataloging-in-Publication Data is available on the Library of Congress website.
ISBN: 9781669033035 (hardcover)
ISBN: 9781669033042 (paperback)
ISBN: 9781669033059 (ebook PDF)

Summary: Welcome to the land of sunflowers: Ukraine! From the sandy coasts of the Black Sea to the vibrant capital of Kyiv, this proud nation is full of history, culture, and beauty. Explore the bountiful crops that earned this Eastern European country its nickname, the "breadbasket of Europe." Learn more about Ukraine's unique history—from former Soviet Union republic to independent nation. Then discover some of the country's most well-known figures, including President Volodymyr Zelenskyy. Along with bright, bold photographs, celebrated author Oksana Lushchevska shares the treasures of her beloved home country, taking young readers beyond the headlines and into the heart of Ukraine.

Editorial Credits
Editor: Julie Gassman; Designer: Heidi Thompson; Media Researcher: Jo Miller;
Production Specialist: Tori Abraham

Printed and bound in the USA. PO5120

TABLE OF CONTENTS

WELCOME TO UKRAINE!

Welcome to the land of sunflowers: Ukraine. Beneath the blue skies, the sunflowers bloom! Millions of the bright yellow flowers grow all over the land. Their sweet scent goes up, up, up to the mountains . . . and down, down, down to the seas. Blooming from summer to fall, sunflowers look like masterful paintings. For Ukrainians, the sunflower is a symbol of peace.

Ukraine is a large country located in Eastern Europe famous for its rich history and fertile soil. It is a country with deep cultural roots, a diverse natural environment, and unique traditions. Ukraine's history, delicious dishes, art, and language add to the country's beauty and complexity. Discover the treasures that make Ukrainians so proud.

NATIONAL SYMBOLS OF UKRAINE

FLAG: Two equal blue and yellow horizontal bands. Blue represents the sky. Yellow represents the wheat fields.

EMBLEM: A golden trident on a blue shield

FLOWER: Sunflower

BIRD: White stork

ANIMAL: Nightingale *(right)*

DANCE: Hopak

FOOD: Borscht

DRESS: Embroidered shirt

THE POWER OF SUNFLOWERS

Sunflowers stand for prosperity, happiness, and good luck. Ukrainian people love sunflowers. They grow them everywhere. Some grow them in fields for tasty sunflower oil. Others grow them in gardens to tempt bees to pollinate plants. Some prefer to plant sunflowers in their yards for delightful bouquets. Others grow sunflowers for snacking. Have you ever tried sunflower seeds as a snack?

The sunflower has a magical power. Grow it by your house and see for yourself: It will gather the sunshine for you! The sunflower is a true jewel of a yard or balcony. Oh, and don't forget to use a special saying or poem while watering your sunflower. Your sunflower will surely enjoy it.

HOW TO PLANT A SUNFLOWER

DIRECTIONS

STEP 1: In the spring, find a sunny spot with direct sunlight. Prepare the soil. Organic potting soil or homemade compost work the best.

STEP 2: Moisten your soil.

STEP 3: Gently push the sunflower seed into the soil no more than one inch deep.

STEP 4: Cover the sunflower seed with dirt. Press down firmly.

STEP 5: Give your seed plenty of room to grow. Water the sunflower seed daily, but don't overwater it.

Now, remember the special saying? Here's one to try. Use this short Ukrainian poem while watering your sunflower:

FALL, RAIN, FALL

Fall, rain, fall,
Fall for all.
Fall as a treat,
I will cook you a beet.
I'll put treat on a tree.
There, there it will be!
The dove will eat it all.
The rain will fall and fall.
When the dove flies away,
The rain will bring a new day.
Fall rain for growing,
Grow big for showing!

A VAST AND DIVERSE LAND

Ukraine has a zillion diverse landscapes that make it unique. It is known for the high lush Carpathian Mountains in the west. The broad sandy coasts of the Black Sea and the Sea of Azov are full of beautiful beaches. The scenic peninsula of Crimea is famous for its rich culture and resorts. There are big grassy plains and dense green forests all across the country. Indeed, Ukraine is vast and diverse.

Ukraine is the second largest country in Europe. It sits between Poland and Russia, between Western Europe and Asia. This position often played a crucial role in Ukraine's development. Historical events unfolded in the territory of Ukraine just because of its geographical location. Ukraine often served as a shield for Europe against many invasions by their eastern neighbors.

The flatlands in the east and south are famous for their fertile "black earth." Ukraine is cold in the winter and warm in the summer. This climate is good for growing a variety of plants. The rich soil makes Ukraine the biggest producer and exporter of many agricultural products. Leading crops include sugar beets, sunflower seeds, flax seeds, vegetables, fruit, dairy products, and, of course, wheat. Ukraine is known as the "breadbasket of Europe." Many countries have wheat-based foods and treats thanks to Ukraine!

Ukraine exports wheat all over the world.

Bread, pies, buns, and dumplings—all delicious wheat products—are part of Ukrainian food traditions. Let's enjoy a tasty treat through a Ukrainian folktale.

ROOSTER AND TWO MICE: UKRAINIAN FOLKTALE

There once lived two mice, Twist and Turn, and a rooster, Cock-a-Doodle-Doo. The mice just loved to relax, while the rooster got up at dawn, woke everyone up with a song, and went to work.

Once the rooster was sweeping the yard and found a spike of wheat.

"Twist and Turn," cried the rooster, "who will make a pie?"

"Not me!" one answered.

"Not me!" said the other.

"Oh well," the rooster said and set to work.

The little mice just kept playing.

The rooster threshed the spike, put the bag of wheat grains on his shoulder, and went to the mill. Meanwhile, the mice had lots of fun.

Later, the rooster brought back the flour and started making pies. All the little mice did was sing and dance.

When the pies were ready, the rooster removed them from the oven and laid them out on the table.

The mice were already there, waiting for pie!

The rooster said, "Wait a minute! Tell me who made the pies?"

"You," the little mice said very softly.

"And what did you do?"

What did the mice have to say? Nothing. They left the table, and the rooster did not ask them to stay. Who would treat such lazy mice with pies?

Many Ukrainians enjoy bread on its own or made into sandwiches. And, of course, bread is often served with the most popular Ukrainian dish—borscht, a special beet soup. But what do Ukrainians drink with their mouthwatering bread and pies? Uzvar!

The beets in borscht give it a dark red color.

Uzvar is a national Ukrainian beverage made with dried fruits. While cooking it, some Ukrainian chefs add certain spices. You can add some cinnamon, star anise, and nutmeg. Or try popular Ukrainian chef Yevhen Klopotenko's choice and add some rosemary! It will give your drink a fresh flavor.

UZVAR WITH ROSEMARY

INGREDIENTS

1 pound of dried fruit and berries (Traditional choices include apples, pears, and prunes, but choose your favorites.)

2-3 tablespoons of honey or sugar

4 rosemary sprigs

DIRECTIONS

STEP 1: Rinse dried fruits. Put them in a pot with 3 quarts of cold water. With an adult's help using a stove, bring it to a boil.

STEP 2: Let the water boil for about 10 minutes. Add the honey or sugar. Remove the pot from the heat. Add the rosemary to the pot. Put a lid on and set it aside until cool.

STEP 3: Pour uzvar liquid in a glass. Put the fruit on a plate. Include some bread with your serving to make this a delicious meal!

HISTORY OF UKRAINE

The story of Ukraine dates back to the earliest days of settlement, around 32,000 years ago. Various groups of people have lived in present-day Ukraine. The most famous early group were the Trypillians. These people grew crops. They made pottery. They built beautiful houses along the rivers, establishing the largest settlements in Europe and possibly the world, at that time.

A later group that lived there were the Scythians. The Scythians were known for being brave warriors and were among the first people to learn how to ride horses. They traded grains and goods with the Greeks.

In the 6th and the 7th centuries CE the Dnipro River banks were populated by Slavic tribes, the ancestors of the modern Ukrainians.

Trypillian pottery was used to store grain.

HISTORICAL TIMELINE

879 CE—Founding of the first independent state in the area of Ukraine called Kyivan Rus'

988—Volodymyr the Great introduces Orthodox Christianity to Ukraine.

1240—Invasion of Ukraine by the Mongol Empire of East Asia

1300s–1400s—Polish–Lithuanian state takes control of the Ukrainian territory.

1600s—Cossacks emerge and establish an independent state called Hetmanate.

1700s—Russian Empire takes control of Ukraine.

1800s—Russia bans the Ukrainian language, but strong cultural development of Ukraine takes place.

1918—Ukraine declares its independence from the Russian Empire and establishes an independent country.

1921—Soviet Red Army conquers Ukraine and makes it part of the Union of Soviet Socialist Republics (USSR). Of these republics, Russia is the largest.

1932—Soviet policies and decisions are aimed at preventing people of Ukraine from growing and receiving food. This caused 3.9 million Ukrainians to die in the human-created famine called Holodomor.

1991—Ukraine formally declares independence after the collapse of the USSR.

2013—Euromaidan Revolution protests cancellation of trade agreement with European Union

2014—Russia takes control of the Crimean Peninsula and launches a war against Ukraine in the Donbas region. Russian operators bribe, arm, and lie to people to spark riots against the Ukrainian government.

2019—Volodymyr Zelenskyy wins the presidential election.

2022—Russia launches full-scale war against Ukraine.

Volodymyr the Great

Monument to
Hetman of Ukraine

Volodymyr Zelenskyy

THE COSSACKS: HEROIC WARRIOR-DEFENDERS

Who were the Cossacks? The word *Cossack* means someone who is free. Indeed, these people were free. The Cossacks were warrior-defenders of their people's freedom, language, and traditions.

The Cossacks lived along the riverbanks and established camps where they fished, hunted, kept bees, and traded goods. They also liked to create art and to perform a special warrior dance, the hopak.

The Cossacks were known not only for their warrior skills and rebellious spirits, but for their sense of style! They wore a linen shirt, red or blue baggy pants, a wide belt, and high boots.

Traditional Cossacks are remembered at the Festival of Ukrainian Cossacks in Kyiv.

But the most stylish thing was their haircut! Ukrainian Cossacks shaved their heads, but in the middle of their scalps they left a long tuft of hair called oseledets. (The word *oseledets* means "herring," a type of fish, in Ukrainian.)

TODAY'S COSSACKS

Cossack spirit lives in all Ukrainian people to this day, and if someone calls you a Cossack, it is a real compliment! These strong leaders of Ukraine represent the Cossacks of today.

President Volodymyr Zelenskyy

The Diplomatic Defender Cossack

Volodymyr Zelenskyy is the president of Ukraine. He was elected in 2019. His quote, "Light will overcome darkness," inspires Ukrainians. They remember this while defending their freedom.

Vitali Klitschko

The Champion Boxer Cossack

The mayor of Kyiv is a world-famous champion boxer. Vitali Klitschko is very strong in both his fist and spirit. No wonder kids want to take pictures with him! This mayor is a superman of his people.

Ukraine has been an independent country since 1991. Ukrainians declared their independence on August 24 of that year. Ukraine became a country where people can finally speak their language and be free.

After gaining independence, people developed their economy and culture. They continue to preserve and cherish it. It is not easy for Ukrainians because the neighboring country of Russia still tries to take some territory back under its control. But remember the Cossack spirit? Yes, Ukrainians call upon this spirit as they strive to protect their land and independence.

Ukrainians worked to protect monuments in Kyiv from being damaged by Russian weapons in 2022. They buried statues in sandbags.

PEOPLE AND CULTURE

The people of Ukraine enjoy going to concerts and singing songs. Ukrainians also love traditional and contemporary dances. *Dancing With the Stars* might easily unite the family by the TV on a weekend. Ballet also attracts attention. The success of Ukrainian prima ballerina Kateryna Kukhar inspires many children to enroll in dance and ballet schools across the country.

But most of all, Ukrainians like to celebrate holidays! One of the most important holidays is Independence Day on August 24. This day is widely celebrated not only in Ukraine but by Ukrainians all over the world.

A military parade marks Independence Day in Kyiv.

In Kyiv and other large cities and towns people go to the main squares, where they enjoy concerts and fireworks. Kids in schools always get ready for this holiday by reading Ukrainian poems and singing traditional songs.

LEARN UKRAINIAN!

Hi: Привіт (pre-VEET)

Goodbye: До побачення (DOE poh-bah-cheh-nyah)

Bye: Па-па (PA-pa)

Please: Будь ласка (BOOD LAH-skah)

Thank you: Дякую (DAH-koo-yoo)

How are you?: Як справи? (YAHK sprah-vyeh)

Very good: Дуже добре (DOO-zhay DOE-bray)

Excuse me: Вибачте (vyee-BAHCH-teh]

Yes: Так (TAHK)

No: Ні (NEE)

A Christmas tree stands in front of the famous Sophia Cathedral in Kyiv.

RELIGIOUS CELEBRATIONS

Many Ukrainians are Eastern Orthodox Christians. Orthodox Christians celebrate Christmas on January 7. Ukrainians usually begin their celebrations on Christmas Eve, January 6. There is a belief that a Ukrainian Christmas Holy Supper should begin on Christmas Eve when the first star appears in the sky. The whole family gathers to begin celebrating at that time.

Traditionally, Ukrainians threw kutia on their ceilings on Christmas Eve. The more kutia that stuck, the more luck they would have in the coming year.

Holy Supper is always meatless and consists of twelve courses. The most important dish is kutia. It is a delicious dish of cooked wheat, honey, nuts, raisins, and poppy seeds. People also like to serve traditional Ukrainian borscht (beet soup), varenyky (dumplings filled with potatoes or cabbage), holubtsi (cabbage rolls), and uzvar, of course!

On Christmas Day, Ukrainians visit their friends and sing lots of Christmas carols, which are called koliada. You might already know one popular Christmas song—"Carol of the Bells." In Ukrainian, children call this song "Shchedryk," which means "Bountiful Evening."

Ukrainians use wax to create detailed designs on pysanky.

Easter is another important holiday for Ukrainians. One Ukrainian Easter tradition is well-known around the world—pysanky, or Easter eggs. Ukrainian pysanky are typically decorated with detailed patterns found in traditional Ukrainian folk art. These unique designs symbolize a gift of life and wishes of protection and love.

There is a variety of colors and patterns to choose from for creating your own pysanky. You can use special dyes and designs, or you can simply dye your eggs in many natural colors. Naturally colored eggs are called krashanka. The word *krashanka* means krasyty / красити: "to make beautiful or paint."

COLOR EGGS NATURALLY

The favorite way to color Easter eggs is by using onion skins. Let's do it!

INSTRUCTIONS

STEP 1: Gather the dried skins of about 10-15 onions, red or golden is preferable. Place the skins in a large pot.

STEP 2: Rinse your eggs and place them in the pot with the onion skins.

STEP 3: Fill the pot with water so eggs are covered. Bring to a boil, then simmer for 20 minutes.

STEP 4: Check eggs for color.

STEP 5: When ready, carefully remove eggs. Let them cool, then enjoy!

Special tools and a lot of patience are used to create the designs on pysanky.

READING AND ART RECREATION

Like children in many parts of the world, Ukrainian kids love to read. Reading is such a large part of Ukrainian culture that there is a tale about an Old Lion and children's books. The story takes place in Lviv, designated as a City of Literature. The tale goes like this: There is an old lion in Lviv, who lives in the Old City. This lion likes to visit favorite sightseeing spots and write children's books. Ukrainian children love this lion.

This legend helped launch another fabulous tradition. A children's reading festival called BookMania takes place in Lviv every spring. Can you meet an Old Lion over there? No doubt. You can even read a book or two with him!

Interestingly, Lviv is the city with a large collection of lion statues. Lions are not native to Ukraine, but you can find a lot of lion images, created by the famous Ukrainian artist Mariya Prymachenko.

Lion statues are found all over Lviv, but one of the most famous is found at city hall.

MEET MARIYA PRYMACHENKO

Mariya Prymachenko (1909–1997) was a Ukrainian folk-art painter. She was famous for her naïve style, which means she liked to paint like kids, with imaginative, bright, and colorful designs. During her childhood Mariya was ill with polio, a painful disease. To make herself feel better, she looked for the beauty in nature and animals. Mariya never studied art. But she learned that if one has paper, brushes, and colors, and a possibility to be in nature, masterpieces can be created. Mariya painted a lot of different animals, but lions were her favorite. Try drawing a lion like Mariya!

Mariya Prymachenko's paintings have inspired other art pieces and even a playground in Kyiv!

Ukrainians keep their traditions alive while looking toward the future.

Ukraine is truly a country full of surprises. Due to its geographical location, Ukraine has been influenced by other nations and cultures. Many times, it has also been threatened and even disappeared, becoming a part of another country. Yet, Ukraine has emerged stronger. It continues to develop as a full member of the world community by honoring the past, while looking to the future. And that future is bright, sunflower bright!

UKRAINE FACT FILE

OFFICIAL NAME: Ukraine

POPULATION: 43,528,136

LAND AREA: 233,062 square miles (603,628 square kilometers)

CAPITAL: Kyiv

MONEY: Ukrainian hryvnia (UAH)

GOVERNMENT: Republic, with an elected president

OFFICIAL LANGUAGE: Ukrainian

NATURAL RESOURCES: Coal, natural gas, oil, timber, farmland

UKRAINIAN ALPHABET

The Ukrainian language is an East Slavic language. It can be traced back to the late 800s to the 1200s. The language survived many bans throughout history and finally developed into the modern Ukrainian language. It uses the Ukrainian alphabet. See how its letters compare to the letters you are used to.

А а	Б б	В в	Г г	Ґ ґ
A	B	V	H	G
Д д	Е е	Ё ё	Ж ж	З з
D	E	YE	ZH	Z
И и	І і	Ї ї	Й й	К к
Y	I	YI	J	K
Л л	М м	Н н	О о	П п
L	M	N	O	P
Р р	С с	Т т	У у	Ф ф
R	S	T	U	F
Х х	Ц ц	Ч ч	Ш ш	Щ щ
R	S	T	U	F
Ъ ъ	Ю ю	Я я		
R	YU	YA		

INDEX

ABOUT THE AUTHOR

Oksana Lushchevska is a Ukrainian writer and translator. She is an active member of PEN Ukraine, an organization dedicated to protecting the freedom of speech and promoting literature in Ukraine. Oksana is the author of 44 children's and young adult books. Her books have been awarded a number of Ukrainian children's literature awards. Oksana has a PhD in education and taught children's literature courses at the University of Georgia, USA. She is currently a children's literature consultant. Oksana lives in Charlotte, North Carolina, USA.